contents

D1341030

Key

- Addition and Subtraction
- Multiplication and Division
- Shape and Measure
- Fractions and Decimals
- Mixed Operations

How to use this book

Read the instructions carefully before each set of questions.

The first page of each section will have a title telling you what the next few pages are about.

Your teacher may tell you to GRAB something that might help you answer the questions.

Sometimes a character will give you a tip.

Some pages will show you an example or model.

Solve these word problems.

1 24 fish are caught in a net. The chef needs 8 fish to make a fish pie. How many pies can the chef make from today's catch? If a pie feeds 10 people, how many people can the chef cook for?

2 The next day, 56 fish are caught in the net. How many pies can the chef make from this catch? How many people can the chef cook for?

3 Chews cost 12p each. Mrs Jones buys one chew for each of her 8 children. How much change from £1 does she get?

4 Mr Robson buys some 6p sweets. He has 85p. He wants to give 2 sweets each to his 7 children. Does he have enough money and if so, will he get change?

5 Each table in a classroom has 4 small chairs around it, apart from the teacher's table which has only one large chair. There are 17 tables in the classroom altogether. How many small chairs are there? If half of them are not empty, how many are empty?

6 In a different classroom there are 78 chairs. If 5 chairs are put round each table, leaving 3 chairs over, how many tables are there altogether?

Remember to use RNCA!

THINK Work with a partner to write two word problems like these.

- I am confident with using multiplication and division to solve word problems.

78

Tenths and equivalent fractions

Write the fraction for each colour.

GRAB! Sticks of 10 in red and blue

1  red = $\frac{\Box}{10}$ blue = $\frac{\Box}{10}$

2 red = $\frac{\Box}{10}$ blue = $\frac{\Box}{10}$

3 red = $\frac{\Box}{10}$ blue = $\frac{\Box}{10}$

4 red = $\frac{\Box}{10}$ blue = $\frac{\Box}{10}$

5 red = $\frac{\Box}{10}$ blue = $\frac{\Box}{10}$

6 red = $\frac{\Box}{10}$ blue = $\frac{\Box}{10}$

7 Which sheet of stickers has one-half in red?

8 Which sheet of stickers has one-fifth in blue?

THINK Write an addition of three fractions which gives the answer 1.

- I am confident with tenths.

79

THINK questions will challenge you to think more about the maths on the page.

Choose a traffic light colour to say how confident you are with the maths on the page.

Each area of maths has its own colour.

Add and subtract using number facts

Solve these mentally using number facts. Write the number facts that helped you.

1 487 + 5 = ☐ ○ ○

7 + 5 = 12

You could add 9 by adding the 5 and then adding the 4!

2 375 + 9 = ☐

3 283 + 6 = ☐

4 726 + 8 = ☐

5 577 + 7 = ☐

6 683 + 4 = ☐

7 848 + 5 = ☐

8 239 + 7 = ☐

9 418 + 9 = ☐

10 476 + 7 = ☐

11 885 + 6 = ☐

12 943 + 8 = ☐

THINK Write a question adding a 1-digit number to a 3-digit number where the number fact 6 + 3 = 9 will be helpful.

○
○ **I am confident with adding 3-digit and 1-digit**
○ **numbers using number facts.**

Subtract 5 from each of these numbers.

1 118   **3** 485   **5** 182

2 307   **4** 624   **6** 741

Subtract 7 from each of these numbers.

7 589   **9** 250   **11** 311

8 467   **10** 862   **12** 253

Subtract 9 from each of these numbers.

13 589   **16** 211   **19** 308

14 367   **17** 785   **20** 702

15 724   **18** 324   **21** 401

 **THINK** When subtracting 9, you can round it to 10 and then adjust. Write a rule to teach someone how to subtract 9.

I am confident with subtracting 1-digit numbers from 3-digit numbers mentally.

5

Use your number facts to solve these.

1. 183 + 5 = ☐

2. 245 – 4 = ☐

3. 357 + 2 = ☐

4. 378 – 6 = ☐

5. 481 + 8 = ☐

6. 437 – 5 = ☐

7. 422 + 7 = ☐

8. 529 – 8 = ☐

9. 587 – 7 = ☐

10. 566 + 4 = ☐

11. 677 – 8 = ☐

12. 619 + 5 = ☐

13. 777 – 9 = ☐

14. 796 + 5 = ☐

15. 884 – 9 = ☐

16. 997 + 8 = ☐

THINK When adding or subtracting 9, you can round it to 10 and then adjust. Write a rule to teach someone how to add 9.

I am confident with adding and subtracting 1-digit numbers to or from 3-digit numbers mentally.

Copy and complete these additions and subtractions.

GRAB! Multiples of 10, bonds to 60, 70, 80, 90 and 100 poster

① 645 + 30 = ☐

② 433 + 60 = ☐

③ 217 + 80 = ☐

④ 853 + 40 = ☐

⑤ 782 + 50 = ☐

⑥ 674 + 70 = ☐

⑦ 295 − 50 = ☐

⑧ 883 − 70 = ☐

⑨ 261 − 60 = ☐

⑩ 794 − 30 = ☐

⑪ 225 − 30 = ☐

⑫ 342 − 80 = ☐

 **THINK**

☐45 + ☐0 = ☐

Can you solve this problem, then write and complete four others where the coloured digits are the same as each other?

I am confident with adding and subtracting multiples of 10 to and from 3-digit numbers.

1 827 + 30 = ☐

2 863 − 40 = ☐

3 747 + 80 = ☐

4 634 − 70 = ☐

5 882 + 50 = ☐

6 215 − 50 = ☐

7 543 + 60 = ☐

8 361 − 80 = ☐

9 653 + 70 = ☐

10 666 − 90 = ☐

Solve this problem.

11 There are 254 occupied seats on a train. At the next stop 60 people get off. How many people remain on the train?

 **THINK** Complete these additions:

232 + 20   343 + 30   454 + 40

Write the next four additions in the sequence. What pattern do you notice in the 10s digit? Can you spot any other patterns?

I am confident with adding and subtracting multiples of 10 to and from 3-digit numbers.

8

1 Rory works as a waiter in a restaurant. Last month he earned £428 plus £90 in tips. How much did he earn altogether?

2 In a game of darts Poppy's score is 347. She throws three darts and now must subtract 60 from her score. What is her score now?

3 At St Michael's school there are 40 members of staff and 584 children. When all the staff and children sit in the hall, how many people are there in total?

4 Claire and Mark are getting married. They have 165 guests. Mark has ordered 8 packs of napkins. There are 10 napkins in a pack. How many more packs must they order to make sure they have enough?

 THINK

$123 + 30$ $234 + 40$ $345 + 50$

Continue this sequence. Describe the pattern in the 10s digit. Is there a pattern in the 1s digit? Can you see any other patterns?

Try $321 + 10$, $432 + 20$, and so on. What patterns can we expect? Try other 3-digit numbers with consecutive digits.

I am confident with adding and subtracting multiples of 10 to and from 3-digit numbers.

ordering fractions

Write each set of three fractions in order from smallest to largest.

1 $\frac{3}{3}$ $\frac{1}{3}$ $\frac{2}{3}$

2 $\frac{4}{5}$ $\frac{2}{5}$ $\frac{1}{5}$

3 $\frac{1}{6}$ $\frac{3}{6}$ $\frac{2}{6}$

4 $\frac{5}{8}$ $\frac{1}{8}$ $\frac{6}{8}$

5 $\frac{3}{4}$ $\frac{1}{4}$ $\frac{2}{4}$

6 $\frac{5}{10}$ $\frac{9}{10}$ $\frac{3}{10}$

THINK   There are three fractions on this page that are equal to $\frac{1}{2}$. There is one fraction that is equal to I. Can you find them?

○
○   **I am confident with ordering fractions with the**
○   **same denominator.**

10

1. $\frac{3}{8}$ $\frac{1}{8}$ $\frac{7}{8}$ $\frac{4}{8}$

2. $\frac{1}{10}$ $\frac{9}{10}$ $\frac{5}{10}$ $\frac{7}{10}$

3. $\frac{3}{5}$ $\frac{2}{5}$ $\frac{1}{5}$ $\frac{4}{5}$

4. $\frac{2}{7}$ $\frac{1}{7}$ $\frac{5}{7}$ $\frac{6}{7}$

5. $\frac{2}{9}$ $\frac{4}{9}$ $\frac{8}{9}$ $\frac{1}{9}$

6. $\frac{3}{6}$ $\frac{1}{6}$ $\frac{6}{6}$ $\frac{5}{6}$

7. There are three fractions on this page that are equal to $\frac{1}{2}$. Can you find them?

8. Find a fraction that is equal to 1.

9. Rewrite your answer to question 2 using $\frac{1}{2}$ instead of $\frac{5}{10}$.

$$\frac{3}{10} < \frac{\square}{2} < \frac{7}{10}$$

What number is missing? Write your own missing number comparison using fractions.

I am confident with ordering fractions with the same denominator.

Write these fractions in order from smallest to largest.

1. $\frac{1}{5}$ $\frac{4}{5}$ $\frac{5}{5}$ $\frac{3}{5}$

2. $\frac{3}{7}$ $\frac{5}{7}$ $\frac{1}{7}$ $\frac{6}{7}$

Think what $\frac{1}{2}$ or $\frac{1}{4}$ would be if they had the same denominator as the other fractions.

3. $\frac{2}{6}$ $\frac{1}{2}$ $\frac{5}{6}$ $\frac{1}{6}$

4. $\frac{4}{10}$ $\frac{9}{10}$ $\frac{1}{10}$ $\frac{1}{2}$

5. $\frac{1}{2}$ $\frac{4}{6}$ $\frac{1}{6}$ $\frac{5}{6}$

6. $\frac{3}{8}$ $\frac{1}{4}$ $\frac{1}{8}$ $\frac{7}{8}$

7. Find the halves on this page and write them as fractions within their own family, for example, $\frac{1}{2} = \frac{3}{6}$.

8. Find a fraction that is equal to 1.

$$\frac{3}{8} < \frac{\square}{4} < \frac{8}{10}$$

What numbers could go in the box?

I am confident with ordering fractions with and without the same denominator.

Multiplying by 2, 3, 4, 5 and 8

These are inputs for the ×2 machine. Write the outputs.

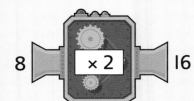

8 | ×2 | 16

1 6   **3** 25   **5** 100

2 9   **4** 20

Here are outputs from the ×2 machine. Write the inputs.

6 8   **7** 100   **8** 14   **9** 30

These are inputs for the ×3 machine. Write the outputs.

10 5   **12** 4   **14** 9

11 8   **13** 7

6 | ×3 | 18

Here are outputs from the ×3 machine. Write the inputs.

15 30   **16** 9   **17** 21   **18** 24

These are inputs for the ×4 machine. Write the outputs.

3 | ×4 | 12

19 4   **21** 7   **23** 6

20 8   **22** 9

Here are outputs from the ×4 machine. Write the inputs.

24 12   **25** 20   **26** 40   **27** 44

I am confident with multiplying by 2, 3 and 4.

These are inputs for the ×3 machine. Write the outputs.

1 6   **3** 12   **5** 7

2 8   **4** 10

Here are outputs from the ×3 machine. Write the inputs.

6 9   **7** 24   **8** 27   **9** 15   **10** 33

These are inputs for the ×4 machine. Write the outputs.

11 5   **13** 9   **15** 11

12 3   **14** 12

5 — × 4 — 20

Here are outputs from the ×4 machine. Write the inputs.

16 16   **17** 32   **18** 48   **19** 400   **20** 80

These are inputs for the ×8 machine. Write the outputs.

3 — × 8 — 24

21 4   **23** 7   **25** 11

22 3   **24** 8

Here are outputs from the ×8 machine. Write the inputs.

26 80   **27** 16   **28** 40   **29** 72   **30** 48

THINK Draw two machines that together do the same job as the machine that multiplies by 8.

I am confident with multiplying by 3, 4 and 8.

These are inputs for the ×8 machine. Write the outputs.

1 7   **2** 9   **3** 12    3 → ×8 → 24

Here are outputs from the ×8 machine. Write the inputs.

4 80   **5** 88   **6** 64   **7** 56   **8** 160

**These are inputs for the ×2 then ×4 machine.
What are the outputs?**

9 3   **11** 6

10 5   **12** 9

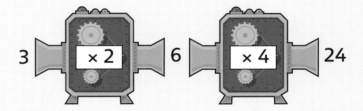

3 → ×2 → 6 → ×4 → 24

**These are inputs for the ×5 then ×4 machine.
What are the outputs?**

13 2   **15** 6

14 4   **16** 8

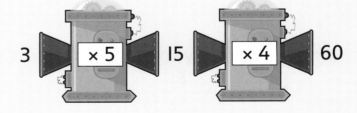

3 → ×5 → 15 → ×4 → 60

17 If each pair of machines was changed into just one machine, what would be written on that machine?

 Design a 2-stage machine which would give an output of 48.

I am confident with multiplying by 2, 3, 4, 5 and 8.

Scaling

Work out the heights of the Gianormous family. Helga is twice as tall as Timmy, and Mum is 4 times as tall as Timmy.

1 If you just know Helga's height, how can you work out Timmy's height?

2 If you just know Helga's height, can you work out Mum's height without working out Timmy's height? Explain how.

3 If you know Mum's height, can you work out Helga's height without working out Timmy's? Explain how.

4 If Timmy is $3\frac{1}{2}$ m tall, how tall is Mum?

5 If Helga is 8m tall, how tall is Timmy? How tall is Mum?

6 If Helga is 1 tree tall, how tall is Timmy? How tall is Mum?

Work out the heights of the Humungous family. Mungo is 5 times the height of little Esme. Dad is 10 times the height of little Esme.

7 If you just know Mungo's height, how can you work out Esme's height?

8 If you just know Mungo's height, can you work out Dad's height without working out Esme's height? Explain how.

9 If you know Dad's height, can you work out Mungo's height without working out Esme's? Explain how.

10 If Esme is $2\frac{1}{2}$ m tall, how tall is Dad?

I am confident with multiplying or dividing to find related heights.

16

Multiples of 10

Write the costs of the masks.

20p

40p

30p

50p

1 3 clown masks

2 5 alien masks

3 6 clown masks

4 3 alien masks

5 2 teddy bear masks

6 7 monkey masks

7 4 teddy bear masks

8 9 monkey masks

9 10 alien masks and 4 monkey masks

10 6 teddy bear masks and 5 clown masks

Copy and complete.

11 3 × 30 = ☐

12 8 × 50 = ☐

13 50 × 5 = ☐

14 5 × 40 = ☐

15 40 × 3 = ☐

16 9 × 30 = ☐

17 6 × 30 = ☐

18 4 × 20 = ☐

19 2 × 60 = ☐

THINK How many of each mask can you buy for £5?

I am confident with multiplying multiples of 10 by 1-digit numbers.

Solve these word problems.

1 Kate bought 5 grapefruits for 30p each. How much change does she have from £2?

2 Matchboxes hold 50 matches. They are sold in packs of 5 boxes. How many matches in a pack? How many packs must I buy to have 1000 matchsticks?

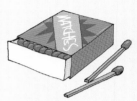

3 The circus seats are in rows of 40. If 140 people try to sit in the front 3 rows, how many people will not be able to get a seat?

4 The Jolly Giant grows 20 cm every week. He is now 310 cm tall. How tall will he be in 4 weeks time?

Copy and write the missing numbers.

5 $3 \times 40 = \square$

6 $\square \times 3 = 180$

7 $80 \times \square = 400$

8 $5 \times 40 = \square$

9 $50 \times \square = 150$

10 $7 \times 500 = \square$

11 $4 \times \square = 120$

12 $\square \times 4 = 240$

13 $9 \times \square = 3600$

 **THINK** Look at these multiplications. Find the numbers that fit. Can you find other pairs like these?

$$\square \times 30 = \square \times 40$$
$$\square \times 50 = \square \times 20$$

- I am confident with multiplying multiples of 10 by 1-digit numbers.

Multiplying using the grid method

$3 \times 25 = \square$

×	20	5	
3	60	15	= 75

Perform these multiplications using the method shown.

1. $4 \times 16 = \square$

2. $6 \times 13 = \square$

3. $3 \times 24 = \square$

4. $17 \times 5 = \square$

5. $7 \times 13 = \square$

6. $24 \times 4 = \square$

7. $3 \times 28 = \square$

8. $4 \times 19 = \square$

9. $16 \times 6 = \square$

10. $5 \times 19 = \square$

Solve these problems.

11. A tube of sweets costs 26p. How much does it cost to buy 3 tubes of sweets?

12. At the school fête a cup of tea costs 17p. The Jones family buy 4 cups of tea. How much do they pay?

 THINK   What are the missing digits?

$$4 \times \square\square = 124$$

○
○ **I am confident with multiplying using the grid method.**
○

19

Perform these multiplications using the grid method.

1 3 × 32 = ☐

2 2 × 38 = ☐

3 3 × 27 = ☐

4 18 × 5 = ☐

5 7 × 14 = ☐

6 26 × 4 = ☐

7 3 × 36 = ☐

8 5 × 27 = ☐

9 21 × 7 = ☐

10 8 × 32 = ☐

Solve these problems.

11 A can of drink costs 38p. How much does it cost to buy 3 cans of drink?

12 Chews cost 6p each. Mrs Jones buys one chew for each child in her class. There are 25 children in her class. How much does Mrs Jones pay?

 THINK

ME × 4 = PET
Each letter is a different digit. Find what digits M, E, P and T stand for.

I am confident with multiplying using the grid method.

Dividing 2-digit and 3-digit numbers by 1-digit numbers

Complete these divisions drawing number lines to help.

1 65 ÷ 5 = ☐ ☐ × 5 = 65

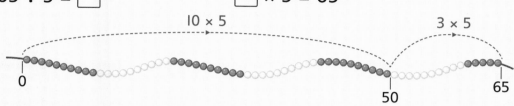

10 × 5   3 × 5

0   50   65

2 45 ÷ 3 = ☐ ☐ × 3 = 45

10 × 3   ☐ × 3

0   30   45

3 51 ÷ 3 = ☐ ☐ × 3 = 51

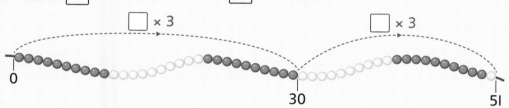

☐ × 3   ☐ × 3

0   30   51

4 52 ÷ 4 = ☐

0   52

5 85 ÷ 5 = ☐

0   85

6 48 ÷ 3 = ☐

0   48

I am confident with dividing 2-digit numbers by 1-digit numbers using a number line.

1   56 ÷ 4 = ☐

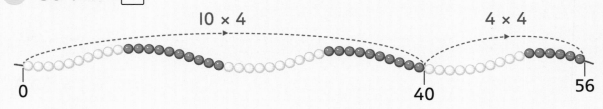

10 × 4   4 × 4

0   40   56

2   104 ÷ 8 = ☐

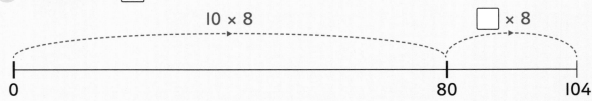

10 × 8   ☐ × 8

0   80   104

3   75 ÷ 5 = ☐

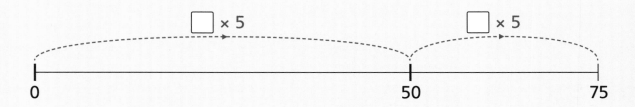

☐ × 5   ☐ × 5

0   50   75

4   42 ÷ 3 = ☐   **8**   57 ÷ 3 = ☐

5   68 ÷ 4 = ☐   **9**   128 ÷ 8 = ☐

6   90 ÷ 5 = ☐   **10**   76 ÷ 4 = ☐

7   112 ÷ 8 = ☐   **11**   144 ÷ 8 = ☐

 A number between 50 and 80 divides by 4 to give an answer ending in 4. What is the number?

I am confident with dividing 2- and 3-digit numbers by 1-digit numbers using a number line.

Complete these divisions.

Draw a number line and jump in chunks to help you.

1 44 ÷ 4 = ☐

2 75 ÷ 5 = ☐

3 54 ÷ 3 = ☐

4 104 ÷ 8 = ☐

5 72 ÷ 4 = ☐

6 63 ÷ 3 = ☐

7 95 ÷ 5 = ☐

8 120 ÷ 8 = ☐

9 92 ÷ 4 = ☐

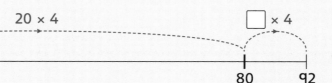

10 78 ÷ 3 = ☐

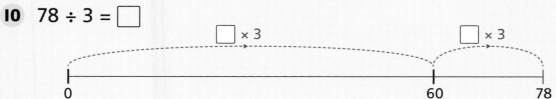

11 125 ÷ 5 = ☐

12 81 ÷ 3 = ☐

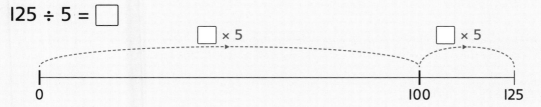

13 Amit has 85 football cards and he sticks them in his book. If 5 cards fit on each page, how many pages do his cards fill?

14 Jennie sees 104 octopus legs in the aquarium! How many octopuses are there?

I am confident with dividing 2- and 3-digit numbers by 1-digit numbers using a number line.

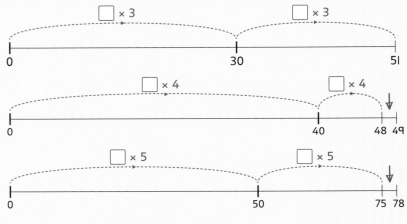

1 $51 \div 3 = \boxed{}$

$\boxed{} \times 3$ $\boxed{} \times 3$

0   30   51

2 $49 \div 4 = \boxed{}$

$\boxed{} \times 4$ $\boxed{} \times 4$

0   40   48 49

3 $78 \div 5 = \boxed{}$

$\boxed{} \times 5$ $\boxed{} \times 5$

0   50   75 78

4

Chunky Chimp has 65 bananas.

He eats 5 bananas a day.

How many days are there until he runs out of bananas?

5

This gorilla has 57 mangos.

He eats 3 mangos a day.

How many days are there until he runs out of mangos?

6

This monkey has 74 figs.

He eats 4 figs a day.

For how many days can he have 4 figs?

How many figs will he have left over?

> **I am confident with dividing 2-digit numbers with and without remainders, using a number line.**

Complete these divisions.

Draw number lines like the first one and jump in chunks to help you.

1 $107 \div 8 =$ ☐

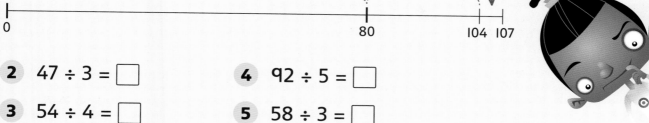

2 $47 \div 3 =$ ☐　　**4** $92 \div 5 =$ ☐

3 $54 \div 4 =$ ☐　　**5** $58 \div 3 =$ ☐

6
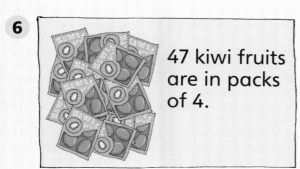
47 kiwi fruits are in packs of 4.

How many packs? How many kiwis are left over?

8
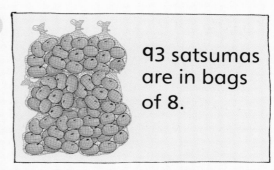
93 satsumas are in bags of 8.

How many bags? How many satsumas are left over?

7

77 bananas are in bunches of 5.

How many bunches? How many bananas are left over?

9

77 pears are in bags of 4.

How many bags? How many pears are left over?

 Write a division word problem for your partner to solve.

I am confident with dividing 2-digit numbers with remainders, using a number line.

Complete these divisions.

1 137 ÷ 5 = ☐

☐ × 5   ☐ × 5   ☐

0   100   135   137   r

2 97 ÷ 4 = ☐

☐ × 4   ☐ × 4   ☐

0   80   96   97   r

3 74 ÷ 3 = ☐

0   60   72   74

4 130 ÷ 8 = ☐

0   80   128   130

5 175 ÷ 8 = ☐

0   160   168   175

6  147 felt-tipped pens are in packs of 5.

How many packs? How many felt-tipped pens are left over?

7  98 crayons are in packs of 4.

How many packs? How many crayons are left over?

8 85 highlighter pens are in packs of 3.

How many packs? How many highlighter pens are left over?

9  86 rubbers are in packs of 4.

How many packs? How many rubbers are left over?

10 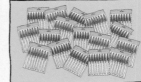 102 ballpoint pens are in packs of 8.

How many packs? How many ballpoint pens are left over?

11  163 sticky notes are in packs of 8.

How many packs? How many sticky notes are left over?

⋮ **I am confident with dividing 2- and 3-digit numbers with remainders, using a number line.**

Multiplying 2-digit numbers by 1-digit numbers

Complete these multiplications.

1 34 × 3 = ☐

×	30	4
3	90	12

= ☐

2 4 × 43 = ☐

×	40	3
4		

= ☐

3 3 × 26 = ☐

4 48 × 4 = ☐

5 5 × 33 = ☐

6 38 × 4 = ☐

7 23 × 8 = ☐

8 3 × 42 = ☐

Solve these problems.

9 There are 28 cars in a traffic jam. Each car has 5 people in it. How many people are stuck in the traffic jam?

10 32 model cars need 4 wheels each. How many wheels are needed?

11 Emil, Kara and Sarah are baking for their school cake sale. They each bake 36 cakes. How many cakes do they have to sell altogether?

I am confident with multiplying 2-digit numbers by I-digit numbers using the grid method.

Complete these multiplications.

1. 62 × 4 = ☐

2. 74 × 6 = ☐

3. 8 × 55 = ☐

4. 68 × 3 = ☐

5. 84 × 8 = ☐

6. 6 × 93 = ☐

7. 65 × 5 = ☐

8. 72 × 4 = ☐

9. 6 × 88 = ☐

10. 94 × 3 = ☐

Solve these problems.

11. How many legs do 56 horses have altogether?

12. Clive cycled 66 kilometres every week for 3 weeks. How far did he cycle in total?

13. There are 52 cards in each pack of playing cards. How many cards are there in 6 packs of playing cards?

14. A supermarket sells tins of tuna in packs of 3. How many tins are on the shelf if there are 35 packs?

☐ × 3 is 15 more than ☐ × 4.

What numbers could be in the boxes?

I am confident with multiplying 2-digit numbers by 1-digit numbers using the grid method.

28

Look at this example.

4 × 37

Round 37 ⟶ 40

Write the estimate: 4 × 40 = 160

Now use the grid.

×	30	7	
4	120	28	= 148

Write the exact answer: 4 × 37 = 148

Repeat this process to perform these.

1 5 × 44 = ☐

Don't forget to estimate.

2 3 × 39 = ☐

3 4 × 43 = ☐

4 36 × 3 = ☐

5 8 × 26 = ☐

6 47 × 3 = ☐

7 8 × 35 = ☐

8 23 × 9 = ☐

9 6 × 34 = ☐

10 7 × 42 = ☐

 **THINK**

3 × ☐ = 150

Write a multiplication with an answer of just a little less than 150 and a multiplication with an answer of just a little more than 150.

●
● **I am confident with multiplying 2-digit numbers by**
● **1-digit numbers and estimating the products.**

Pictograms and bar charts

Look at this survey about a school's lunch types.

Dinner type	Number of children
School dinner – meat	12
School dinner – vegetarian	3
Packed lunch – meat	9
Packed lunch – vegetarian	9

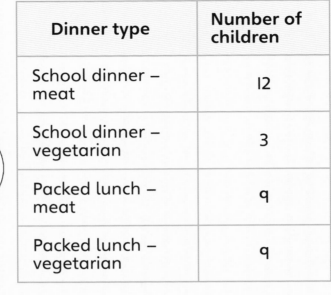

1 Draw a pictogram like the one below to show this information. Each picture is to represent two children.

School dinner – meat	School dinner – vegetarian	Packed lunch – meat	Packed lunch – vegetarian

What picture will you use to represent two children?

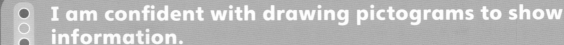

I am confident with drawing pictograms to show information.

1 Copy and complete the frequency table below.
Then draw a bar chart for the information.

Survey of word length in my book						
1-letter words	2-letter words	3-letter words	4-letter words	5-letter words	6-letter words	More than 6 letters

Your bar chart might look like this!

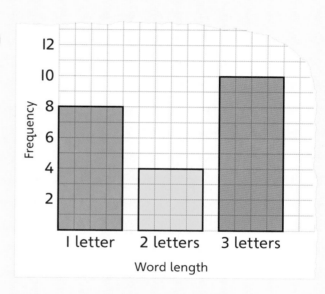

2 What is the most common length of word?

3 What is the least common word length?

4 Which lengths of word occur the same number of times?

5 Is any length of word twice as common as another?

THINK If you did the same survey for name length,
how different would your findings be?

I am confident with drawing bar charts to show information.

Grams and kilograms

Write the weight of each object.

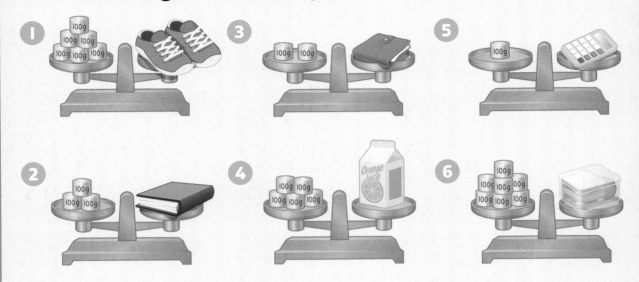

1. 100g 100g 100g 100g 100g 100g
2. 100g 100g 100g
3. 100g 100g
4. 100g 100g 100g 100g 100g
5. 100g
6. 100g 100g 100g 100g 100g 100g 100g

THINK Your bag cannot weigh more than I kg. What objects from above could you put in it?

Estimate the weight of these items in grams or kilograms.

7.

8.

9.

10.

11.

12.

● ○ ○ **I am confident with calculating and estimating weights in grams and kilograms.**

Write each weight in grams.

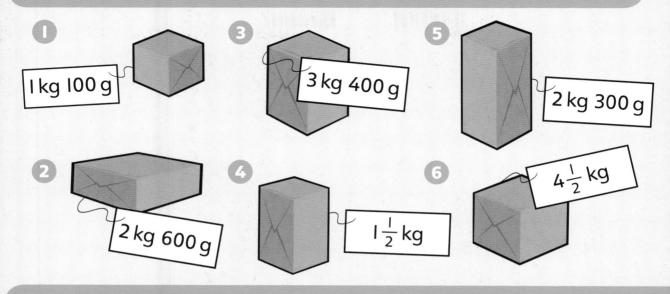

1. 1 kg 100 g
2. 2 kg 600 g
3. 3 kg 400 g
4. $1\frac{1}{2}$ kg
5. 2 kg 300 g
6. $4\frac{1}{2}$ kg

Write the weight of each sack in kilograms and grams.

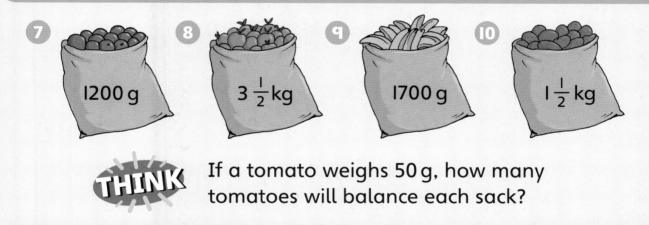

7. 1200 g
8. $3\frac{1}{2}$ kg
9. 1700 g
10. $1\frac{1}{2}$ kg

THINK If a tomato weighs 50 g, how many tomatoes will balance each sack?

Write how many of each item will weigh 1 kilogram.

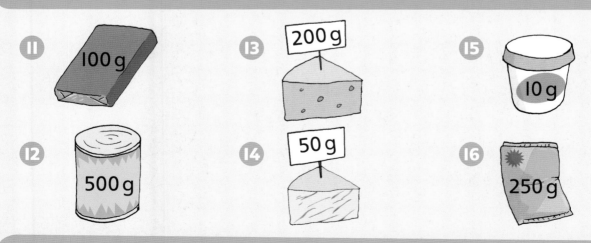

11. 100 g
12. 500 g
13. 200 g
14. 50 g
15. 10 g
16. 250 g

I am confident with calculating weights in grams and kilograms and converting between the two.

Write whether each of these should be measured in grams or kilograms.

For each item above, choose one of the weight labels below to estimate its weight.

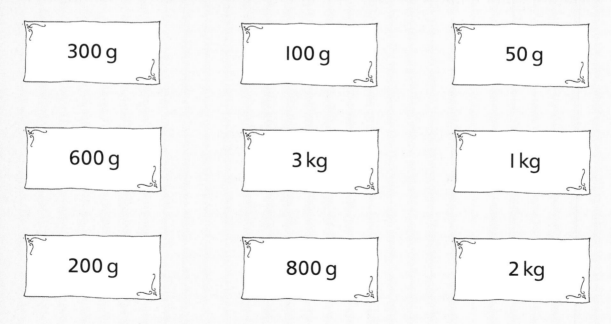

300 g	100 g	50 g
600 g	3 kg	1 kg
200 g	800 g	2 kg

 Find some of the items and weigh them to check your estimates.

I am confident with estimating weights in grams and kilograms.

Write 'likely' or 'unlikely' for each statement.

1. A fully grown cat weighs 25 kilograms.

2. A mouse weighs 25 g.

3. A mobile phone weighs less than a tin of baked beans.

4. A lion weighs 500 g.

5. A teapot full of tea is heavier than a netball.

Read the scales and write the weights.

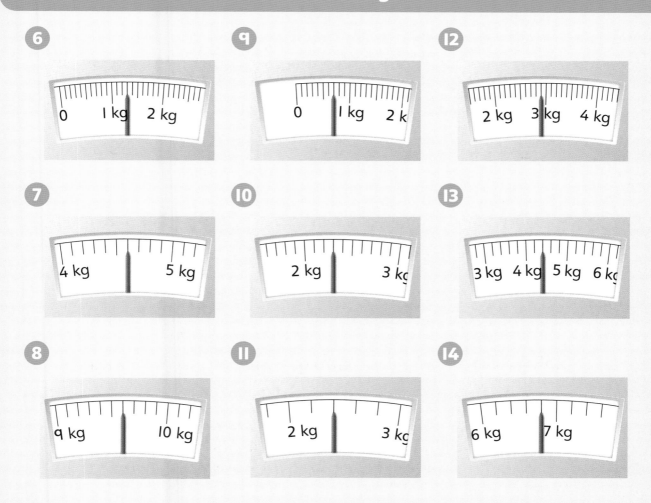

6 0 1 kg 2 kg

9 0 1 kg 2 k

12 2 kg 3 kg 4 kg

7 4 kg 5 kg

10 2 kg 3 kg

13 3 kg 4 kg 5 kg 6 kg

8 9 kg 10 kg

11 2 kg 3 kg

14 6 kg 7 kg

I am confident with estimating weights in grams and kilograms and reading scales.

Adding 2- and 3-digit numbers: mental strategies and written methods

 **THINK** Look at the questions on this page. Estimate which ones will give you an answer greater than 500 and write your answers down.

Complete these additions.

1. 672 + 86 = ☐

2. 815 + 47 = ☐

3. 263 + 72 = ☐

4. 337 + 48 = ☐

5. 708 + 84 = ☐

6. 427 + 56 = ☐

7. 829 + 48 = ☐

8. 261 + 55 = ☐

9. 581 + 63 = ☐

10. 238 + 54 = ☐

11. 488 + 71 = ☐

12. 119 + 63 = ☐

13. 444 + 38 = ☐

14. 181 + 66 = ☐

15. 891 + 41 = ☐

16. 608 + 78 = ☐

I am confident with adding 3-digit and 2-digit numbers mentally.

Complete these additions.

Choose a suitable mental strategy, such as using place value, rounding or counting on in 100s, 10s and 1s.

1 652 + 207 = ☐

2 476 + 119 = ☐

3 348 + 325 = ☐

4 624 + 239 = ☐

5 375 + 204 = ☐

6 128 + 246 = ☐

7 362 + 229 = ☐

8 516 + 350 = ☐

9 245 + 319 = ☐

10 354 + 171 = ☐

11 828 + 161 = ☐

12 473 + 234 = ☐

THINK

468 + 209 = ☐

What method would you use to answer this addition? Rounding? Place value? Or counting on the 100s, 10s and then 1s?

 **I am confident with adding 3-digit numbers mentally.**

Complete these additions.

1 578 + 321 = ☐

2 327 + 459 = ☐

3 648 + 325 = ☐

4 525 + 267 = ☐

5 734 + 153 = ☐

6 359 + 532 = ☐

7 527 + 321 = ☐

8 476 + 319 = ☐

9 563 + 373 = ☐

10 681 + 219 = ☐

11 823 + 175 = ☐

12 622 + 239 = ☐

13 815 + 214 = ☐

14 945 + 127 = ☐

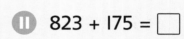

15 One number is 539 more than another number. If the smaller number is 413, what is the larger number?

 **THINK** Choose two additions and check your answers by subtracting one of the numbers you are adding from the answer to see if it gives you the other number.

I am confident with adding 3-digit numbers mentally.

Complete these questions using column addition.

GRAB! Place-value grid

Perform each addition using the method shown.

346 + 278 = ☐

```
  300   40   6
+ 200   70   8
  ─────────────
  100   10
  ─────────────
  600   20   4  = 624
```

1 744 + 128 = ☐

```
  700   40   4
+ 100   20   8
  ─────────────
```

2 435 + 381 = ☐

```
  400   30   5
+ 300   80   1
  ─────────────
```

Now perform these in the same way.

3 578 + 246 = ☐

4 636 + 265 = ☐

5 273 + 261 = ☐

6 356 + 473 = ☐

7 488 + 326 = ☐

8 774 + 169 = ☐

9 583 + 289 = ☐

10 463 + 487 = ☐

THINK Think of three 3-digit + 3-digit additions that you can do without using a written method. Give one to a partner to solve.

I am confident with adding 3-digit numbers using column addition.

Copy and complete these additions using either the expanded or compact column method.

GRAB! Place-value grid

$466 + 238 = \boxed{}$

400	60	6
+ 200	30	8
100	10	
700	0	4 = 704

```
   466
+  238
    11
   704
```

1
```
   635
+  281
_____
```

2
```
   529
+  347
_____
```

3
```
   462
+  375
_____
```

4
```
   324
+  288
_____
```

Now perform these in the same way.

5 $367 + 561 = \boxed{}$

6 $472 + 382 = \boxed{}$

7 $445 + 278 = \boxed{}$

8 $356 + 254 = \boxed{}$

9 $273 + 428 = \boxed{}$

10 $578 + 347 = \boxed{}$

THINK Two numbers have a difference of 467. If the smaller number is 145, what is the larger number?

○
○ **I am confident with adding 3-digit numbers using**
○ **column addition.**

Perform these additions. Estimate the answers first.

① 643
 + 283
 ———

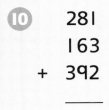

640
+ 290
———
930

② 428
 + 347
 ———

③ 578
 + 237
 ———

④ 573
 + 259
 ———

⑤ 643
 + 278
 ———

⑥ 345
 + 186
 ———

⑦ 467
 + 386
 ———

⑧ 573
 + 418
 ———

⑨ 534
 + 386
 ———

Now perform these in the same way.

⑩ 281
  163
 + 392
 ———

⑪ 267
  175
 + 129
 ———

⑫ 392
  354
 + 216
 ———

⑬ 481
  237
 + 183
 ———

 **THINK**   Think of three 3-digit numbers that add up to 1000.

○
○   **I am confident with adding 3-digit numbers using**
○   **column addition.**

41

Choose a method to solve these additions.

Complete these additions.

1 269 + 320 = ☐

2 408 + 150 = ☐

Solve these using a mental method.

Solve these using column addition.

3 862 + 135 = ☐

4 428 + 343 = ☐

Choose a method to perform these additions.

5 367 + 121 = ☐

6 574 + 284 = ☐

7 333 + 444 = ☐

8 456 + 337 = ☐

9 757 + 140 = ☐

10 578 + 241 = ☐

THINK Write your own mental-method addition and your own column addition. Give them to a partner to solve. Check their answers are correct.

I am confident with choosing a method to add 3-digit numbers.

Complete these additions.

1 586 + 326 = ☐

7 574 + 315 = ☐

Choose to solve these using a mental method or column addition.

2 675 + 217 = ☐

8 824 + 172 = ☐

3 482 + 306 = ☐

9 386 + 285 = ☐

4 593 + 129 = ☐

10 246 + 149 = ☐

5 434 + 247 = ☐

11 674 + 288 = ☐

6 747 + 154 = ☐

12 623 + 165 = ☐

 **THINK** How many of these did you do in your head? How many did you do using column addition? Write an addition which you could answer using a mental method and one which you could answer using the column method.

I am confident with choosing a method to add 3-digit numbers.

Complete these additions.

1 568 + 326 = ☐

7 526 + 297 = ☐

2 463 + 225 = ☐

> Think about what method might be best for each question.

8 158 + 431 = ☐

3 735 + 167 = ☐

9 839 + 114 = ☐

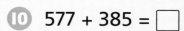

4 463 + 151 = ☐

10 577 + 385 = ☐

5 782 + 139 = ☐

11 143 + 662 = ☐

6 566 + 119 = ☐

12 484 + 483 = ☐

 Find digits to make these additions work.

☐8☐ + ☐☐7 = 999

☐8☐ + ☐☐7 = 911

I am confident with choosing a method to add 3-digit numbers.

Adding several 2- and 3-digit numbers

Perform these additions using the column method.

```
    45              40    5
    68              60    8
+   53         +    50    3
   ____           ─────────────
                  100    50   16  = 166
```

1
```
    53
    21
+   16
   ____
```

3
```
    33
    42
+   15
   ____
```

5
```
    18
    22
    24
+   35
   ____
```

2
```
    42
    15
+   24
   ____
```

4
```
    41
    32
    26
+   35
   ____
```

6
```
    45
    73
+   44
   ____
```

```
    342           300   40    2
     86                 80    6
+   228        +   200   20    8
   ____           ─────────────
                  500   140   16  = 656
```

7
```
    452
     21
+   126
   ____
```

9
```
    353
    412
+    15
   ____
```

11
```
     18
    422
+   284
   ____
```

8
```
    112
    315
+    24
   ____
```

10
```
    133
    422
+   326
   ____
```

12
```
    405
    173
+    44
   ____
```

I am confident with adding several 2- and 3-digit numbers using the column method.

Perform these additions using the column method.

```
    214              214
     83               83
+   312          +   312
 _____               1
                 _____
                    609
```

1
```
    32
    41
    42
+   23
 _____
```

5
```
    371
    132
+   444
 _____
```

9
```
    362
    569
+    64
 _____
```

2
```
    17
    35
    23
+   18
 _____
```

6
```
    228
    269
+   202
 _____
```

10
```
    136
    353
+    53
 _____
```

3
```
    33
    84
    46
+   35
 _____
```

7
```
    533
    227
+    86
 _____
```

11
```
    64
    81
    78
+  103
 _____
```

4
```
    117
    626
+   157
 _____
```

8
```
    374
     68
+   427
 _____
```

12
```
    585
     26
     19
+   204
 _____
```

I am confident with adding several 2- and 3-digit numbers using the column method.

Copy and complete these additions.

1

```
    36
   148
    45
 +  24
 ─────
```

4

```
   378
   272
 + 346
 ─────
```

7

```
   464
   487
 +  63
 ─────
```

2

```
    27
    85
 + 168
 ─────
```

5

```
   258
   139
 + 332
 ─────
```

8

```
   132
   363
 +  58
 ─────
```

3

```
    42
    76
 +  58
 ─────
```

6

```
   483
   126
 +  76
 ─────
```

9

```
    74
    83
 +  48
 ─────
```

Complete these additions.

10 286 + 328 + 128 + 14 = ☐

11 23 + 647 + 251 + 41 = ☐

Solve these word problems.

12 Dave has 62 gold coins, Rani has 82 and Justin has 74. If they discover a stash of 89 more, how many coins do they have altogether?

13 Miss Tidy, the school secretary, is sorting the paper clips. She finds 46 in one box, 87 in another, 129 in a drawer and 63 scattered about her desk. How many paper clips does she have in all?

14 Courtney, Bill and Jamelia raise some money for a charity. Courtney raises £47, Bill raises £48 and Jamelia raises £77. How much do they raise in total?

I am confident with adding several 2- and 3-digit numbers using the column method.

47

Copy and complete these additions.

1
```
    68
    77
    48
+   83
  ____
```

4
```
   286
   179
+  375
  ____
```

7
```
   467
    75
   253
+   58
  ____
```

2
```
    76
    96
    57
+   72
  ____
```

5
```
   395
   474
+  666
  ____
```

8
```
   797
    96
   485
+   88
  ____
```

3
```
    86
    59
    74
+   66
  ____
```

6
```
   986
   578
+  869
  ____
```

Write your own additions using the scores below.

9 Choose four scores to give a total between 180 and 220. Then think of another four ways of doing this.

35   53   28   64   145

27   107   75   15

I am confident with adding several 2- and 3-digit numbers using the column method.

Subtracting 3-digit numbers

Use jottings to complete these subtractions.

1 300 − 265 = ☐

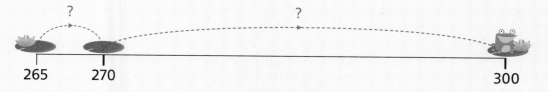

2 800 − 772 = ☐

4 900 − 868 = ☐

3 700 − 683 = ☐

5 600 − 554 = ☐

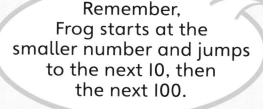

Remember, Frog starts at the smaller number and jumps to the next 10, then the next 100.

Now try these.

6 612 − 595 = ☐

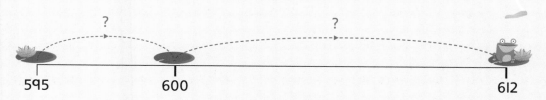

7 408 − 386 = ☐

9 711 − 692 = ☐

8 804 − 787 = ☐

10 508 − 481 = ☐

THINK Frog makes a jump of 4, then a jump of 20 to get to 200. What number did Frog start on?

I am confident with subtracting 3-digit numbers by counting up.

Perform these subtractions by counting up on a number line using Frog.

1 316 − 285 = ☐

5 823 − 792 = ☐

2 385 − 342 = ☐

6 517 − 469 = ☐

3 614 − 578 = ☐

7 931 − 884 = ☐

4 763 − 717 = ☐

8 727 − 681 = ☐

Solve these word problems.

9 Beth has read 164 pages of her book. It has 224 pages, so how many more does she have left to read?

10 Benji has collected 76 stickers. His sticker book has 12 pages with 10 stickers on each page. How many more stickers does he need to collect to fill his sticker book?

⚬⚬⚬ **I am confident with subtracting 3-digit numbers by counting up.**

Choosing a method to solve a problem

Solve these word problems.

How much weight did she lose?

1 Gertie the guinea pig weighed 516 g.

After Gertie lost some weight she weighed 478 g.

2 Kathy buys a guinea pig that weighs 492 g. She carries it home from the pet shop in a 38 g box. How heavy are the box and the guinea pig together?

3 Jake collects football cards. He had 314 cards and was given 143 more. How many does he have now?

4 Sam has 103 cards, but he gives 36 of them to his younger brother. How many does Sam have now?

5 In a garden bird survey, Aswin counted 332 birds on Saturday and 233 birds on Sunday. How many did he count over the weekend altogether?

6 On Saturday Ella counted 283 fewer birds than Aswin did. Aswin counted 332 birds. How many did Ella count?

I am confident with choosing methods to answer addition and subtraction word problems.

Solve these word problems.

1 There is 255 ml of lemonade in a jug. Ted pours a 330 ml can into the jug. How many millilitres of lemonade are there now?

2 A plank of wood is 225 cm long. Mr Amin saws a small piece off the plank, leaving the plank 197 cm long. How long was the piece he sawed off?

3 Kate picks up two tins from a shelf. One tin weighs 425 g and the other weighs 240 g. What do they weigh together?

4 A baby elephant weighed 118 kg at birth. After six weeks it weighed 96 kg more. How much did it weigh then?

5 There is 883 ml of milk left in a carton of milk. The carton, when full, held 925 ml. How much milk has been used?

6 A lorry driver drove 496 km to deliver some metal to a factory. The next day he drove back but, because of diversions, he drove 511 km. How much further did he drive on the way back?

$$348 + 71 = \boxed{}$$

Write a word problem of your own to go with this addition.

Solve these word problems.

1 Harry is 114 cm shorter than his dad.
Harry is 102 cm tall. How tall is his dad?

2 A cruise ship has travelled 177 km of
a 222 km trip. How much further
has it to go?

3 A melon weighs 685 g and an
orange weighs 167 g. How much
do they both weigh together?

4 A large fish tank holds 442 l
of water when full. Billy removes
some water to clean it, leaving
384 l in the tank. He then fills
it to the top again with clean water.
How much clean water did he use?

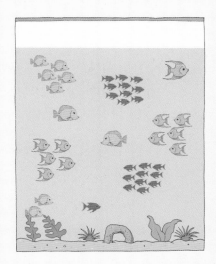

5 Mel makes some fruit cocktail using 373 ml of orange juice
and 420 ml of pineapple juice. How many millilitres of
cocktail are there in total?

6 The bus drops Mrs Eliot 458 m from her house. She has
to walk 394 m up the road and then turn left into a lane.
How far along the lane is her house?

Write your own word problem which
involves subtracting a 3-digit number
and gives an answer of less than 50.

I am confident with choosing methods to answer
addition and subtraction word problems.

53

Solving measures problems with column addition

Copy and complete these additions.

Sam cycles 428 m. Then he runs 246 m. How far does he go in total?

```
  428
+ 246
    1
-----
  674
```

1 Jack swims 175 m. Then he walks 218 m. How far does he go in total?

2 Rani runs 484 m. Then she skips 244 m. How far does she go altogether?

3 Lia swims 567 m. Then she cycles 316 m. How far does she go in total?

4 Connor cycles 624 m. Then he runs 185 m. How far does he go altogether?

5 Jo skips 627 m. Then he hops 157 m. How far does he go?

6 Kieran hops 357 m. Then he runs 278 m. How far does he go altogether?

7 Ed runs 476 m and then hops 369 m. How far does he go?

 **THINK** What might these missing digits be?

```
   □ 2 □
+  4 4 □
     1
-------
   6 7 1
```

I am confident with using column addition involving measures.

Work out the perimeters of these playing fields.

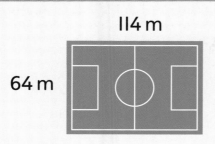

114 m

64 m

Double 64 is 128
Double 114 is 228

```
   128
 + 228
     1
 ————
   356
```

1

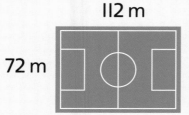

112 m

72 m

3

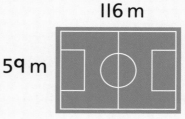

116 m

59 m

2

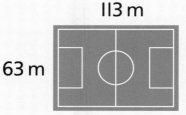

113 m

63 m

4

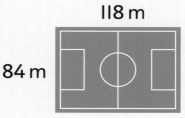

118 m

84 m

Complete these additions.

5
```
   118
 + 157
 ————
```

7
```
   353
 + 427
 ————
```

9
```
   585
 + 284
 ————
```

6
```
   464
 + 372
 ————
```

8
```
   378
 + 435
 ————
```

10
```
   368
 + 267
 ————
```

THINK

If a new playing field can be either 90 m by 110 m or
80 m by 120 m, which will give it the greater perimeter?
Guess first, then work it out. Were you correct?

I am confident with using column addition involving measures.

① Each child swims on three days. How far do they each swim in total?

	Tom	Sara	Sunil
Monday	346 m	348 m	425 m
Tuesday	238 m	392 m	166 m
Wednesday	174 m	194 m	257 m

Find the total weight of these fruits.

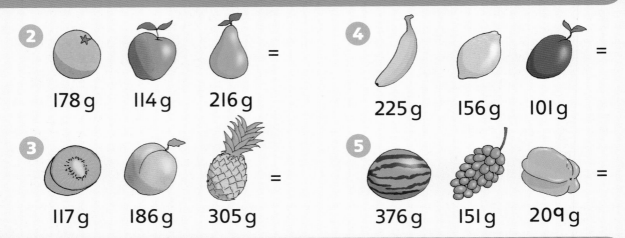

② 178 g   114 g   216 g   =

③ 117 g   186 g   305 g   =

④ 225 g   156 g   101 g   =

⑤ 376 g   151 g   209 g   =

Find the total amount of liquid in these containers.

⑥ 246 ml   119 ml   238 ml   =

⑦ 174 ml   265 ml   132 ml   =

⑧ 492 ml   195 ml   103 ml   =

⑨ 633 ml   127 ml   201 ml   =

THINK Arrange the digits I to 9 to make three 3-digit numbers which add to the largest total possible.

I am confident with using column addition involving measures.

1 How far does each child swim in total?

	Kieran	Lucy	Chen
Monday	486 m	495 m	568 m
Tuesday	578 m	476 m	467 m
Wednesday	375 m	522 m	568 m

Find the total weight of each set of jam jars.

2 396 g 483 g 753 g =

4 649 g 486 g 557 g =

3 187 g 375 g 666 g =

5 678 g 358 g 678 g =

Find the total amount of liquid in these containers.

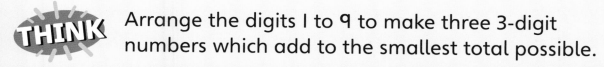

6 696 ml 584 ml 244 ml =

7 889 ml 735 ml 785 ml =

8 Wayne is measuring the water wasted by a dripping tap. On day 1 it leaks 231 ml, on day 2 it leaks 196 ml and on day 3 it leaks 318 ml. How much does it leak in total? Is this more or less than a litre?

9 Matt is making shelves. One shelf is 187 cm long, one is 383 cm and one 45 cm. What is the total length of shelving?

THINK Arrange the digits 1 to 9 to make three 3-digit numbers which add to the smallest total possible.

○
○ **I am confident with using column addition**
○ **involving measures.**

57

Subtraction problems

Solve these word problems.

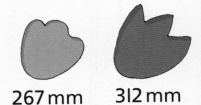

267 mm   312 mm

1 One dinosaur's footprint measures 267 mm. Another dinosaur's footprint measures 312 mm. What is the difference between the size of their footprints?

2 One allosaurus was 532 cm long and another was 495 cm. What was the difference between their lengths?

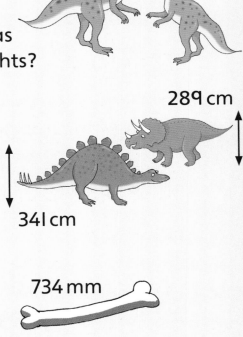

907 kg

878 kg

3 A claosaurus weighed 907 kg and another weighed 878 kg. What was the difference between their weights?

4 A stegosaurus was 341 cm tall. A triceratops was 289 cm tall. How much taller was the stegosaurus than the triceratops?

289 cm

5 An iguanodon was 915 cm long. A triceratops was 829 cm long. How much longer was the iguanodon than the triceratops?

341 cm

6 A dinosaur bone is 672 mm and another bone is 734 mm. How much longer is the larger bone?

734 mm

672 mm

THINK

Joss is 205 cm tall. Harry is 158 cm tall. Measure yourself in centimetres. How much taller is Joss than Harry? What is the difference between your height and Joss' height? What is the difference between your height and Harry's height?

I am confident with problems involving subtracting 3-digit numbers.

Solve these word problems.

1 One dinosaur has a small head. It is 210 mm long. Another dinosaur has a bigger head. It is 304 mm long. What is the difference between the length of the dinosaurs' heads?

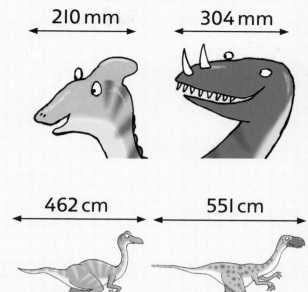

210 mm   304 mm

2 The length of a gallimimus dinosaur was 551 cm. How much longer was it than an ornithomimus, which was 462 cm long?

462 cm   551 cm

3 One claosaurus weighed 907 kg and another weighed 861 kg. What was the difference between their weights?

4 A dryosaurus was 181 cm tall. How much shorter was the dryosaurus than a torosaurus that was 218 cm?

5 Two dinosaur fossils have been found. One is 637 mm long and the other is 564 mm. How much longer is the larger fossil?

6 One dinosaur's footprint measures 946 mm. Another dinosaur's footprint measures 872 mm. What is the difference between the size of their footprints?

THINK The difference between a tiger's footprint and a wildcat's footprint is 55 mm. The tiger's footprint is between 120 and 130 mm. What lengths could the wildcat's footprint be, if it is smaller than the tiger's?

I am confident with problems involving subtracting 3-digit numbers.

Solve these word problems.

519 cm

1 The height of an albertosaurus was 452 cm. How much shorter was it than an allosaurus, which was 519 cm in height?

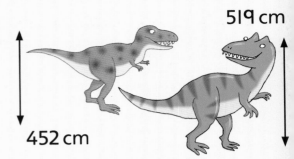

452 cm

2 One maiasaura dinosaur had a skull that was 754 mm long and another had a skull that was 683 mm long. How much longer was the larger skull?

3 A dinosaur bone is 632 mm and another bone is 727 mm. How much shorter is the smaller bone?

4 An explorer found two dinosaur skulls. He measured the distance all the way around the widest part of the two skulls. One skull measured 849 mm and the other measured 763 mm. What is the difference between these two measurements?

5 A claosaurus weighed 917 kg and another weighed 841 kg. What was the difference between their weights?

6 Some dinosaur remains were found from 158 million years ago and from 213 million years ago. How many million years were there between these times?

 Use a ruler to measure your hand span in centimetres. A T-rex's claw span is 45 cm. Work out the difference between your hand span and the T-rex's claw span.

I am confident with solving problems involving subtracting 3-digit numbers.

Choosing a method to add or subtract

Complete these calculations using a mental method.

① 436 + 104 = ☐

③ 704 + 302 = ☐

② 582 + 110 = ☐

④ 46 + 27 = ☐

Complete these calculations using column addition.

⑤ 483 + 217 = ☐

⑥ 328 + 652 = ☐

⑦ 412 + 369 = ☐

Now decide how to complete these calculations.

⑧ 47 + 38 = ☐

⑨ 175 + 203 = ☐

⑩ 156 + 218 = ☐

Complete these calculations by counting up.

⑪ 121 – 87 = ☐

⑫ 306 – 288 = ☐

Complete these calculations by taking away.

⑬ 74 – 29 = ☐

⑭ 426 – 110 = ☐

Now decide how to complete these calculations.

⑮ 206 – 185 = ☐

⑯ 62 – 39 = ☐

THINK You add two 3-digit numbers, where all the digits are the same and all are less than 6. What is the largest total possible?

○
○ **I am confident with adding and subtracting using**
○ **various methods.**

61

Complete three of these calculations in your head and three using column addition. Choose how to complete the other two.

1. 357 + 402 = ☐

2. 642 + 128 = ☐

3. 48 + 37 = ☐

4. 483 + 111 = ☐

5. 174 + 312 = ☐

6. 467 + 217 = ☐

7. 736 + 150 = ☐

8. 385 + 261 = ☐

Complete three of these calculations by counting up and three by taking away. Choose how to complete the other two.

9. 421 – 386 = ☐

10. 121 – 49 = ☐

11. 674 – 103 = ☐

12. 707 – 679 = ☐

13. 632 – 589 = ☐

14. 841 – 350 = ☐

15. Winston has got a best score of 511 on 'Mega-Blast 2'. Today he scored 465. How far off his best score is he?

16. Amy has saved £186. She buys a CD player for £55. How much money does she have left?

Great deal
all CD players
£55!

THINK Two numbers add up to 88. The larger number is 24 more than the smaller. If the smaller number is 32, what is the larger?

I am confident with choosing what method to use to add and subtract.

Complete three of these calculations in your head and three using column addition. Choose how to complete the other three.

1 27 + 25 = ☐   **4** 478 + 256 = ☐   **7** 342 + 201 = ☐

2 429 + 40 = ☐   **5** 420 + 250 = ☐   **8** 624 + 29 = ☐

3 364 + 199 = ☐   **6** 86 + 24 = ☐   **9** 378 + 467 = ☐

Use Frog to work out three of these. Count back to work out three. Choose how to work out the other three.

10 304 – 278 = ☐   **13** 52 – 48 = ☐   **16** 678 – 41 = ☐

11 521 – 40 = ☐   **14** 378 – 201 = ☐   **17** 423 – 378 = ☐

12 62 – 37 = ☐   **15** 98 – 31 = ☐   **18** 321 – 199 = ☐

19 Make up three more additions to do in your head and three more that you would use column addition to answer.

 Two numbers add up to 92. The larger is 24 more than the smaller. If the smaller number is between 30 and 40, what is the larger?

I am confident with choosing what method to use to add and subtract.

Polygon properties

Copy and complete the table to show the information about each shape.

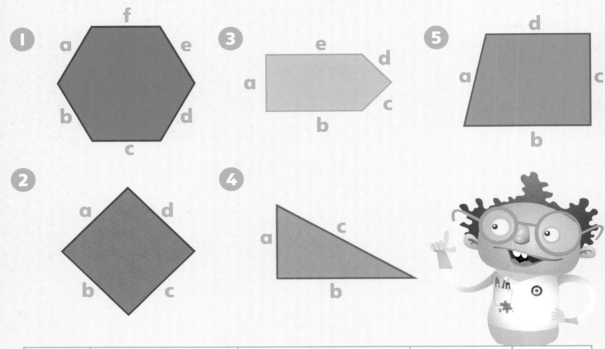

Shape	Pairs of parallel lines	Pairs of perpendicular lines	Horizontal lines	Vertical lines
1	f and c, a and...	none		
2				
3				
4				
5				

THINK Draw a shape with two parallel, two perpendicular, two horizontal and two vertical lines.

 **I am confident with recognising the types of lines used to create polygons.**

Answer the questions about each polygon.

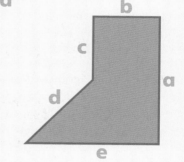

1. How many right angles are there?
2. Are any lines parallel?
3. Which lines are perpendicular?

4. How many pairs of parallel lines are there?
5. Are any lines horizontal?

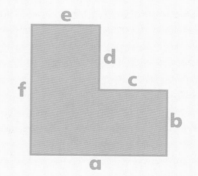

6. Which lines are vertical?
7. Which are horizontal?
8. How many pairs of parallel sides are there?

9. Which lines are parallel to side f?
10. Are the lines parallel to side f vertical or horizontal?
11. How many sides are perpendicular to side f?

12. Copy two symmetrical shapes from this page and draw a line of symmetry in each one.

THINK Draw a shape with two right angles and a line of symmetry. Are any sides perpendicular?

I am confident with recognising the properties of polygons, including lines, angles and symmetry.

Look at the polygons below and answer these questions about each one.

1. How many angles are 90°?

2. Which sides are perpendicular?

3. Which sides are parallel?

4. Is there a line of symmetry?

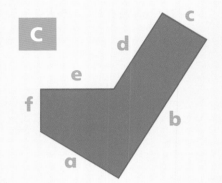

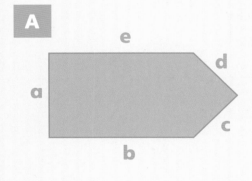

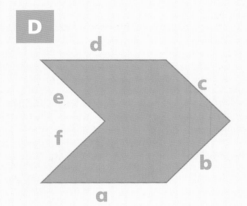

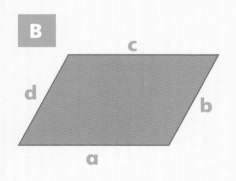

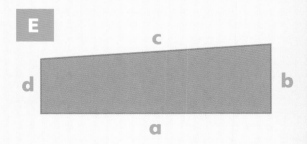

 Draw a shape with a line of symmetry, one right angle and two parallel sides.

I am confident with recognising the properties of polygons, including lines, angles and symmetry.

Measuring perimeters

Write the length of each side in squares. Add the lengths together to calculate the perimeter of each shape.

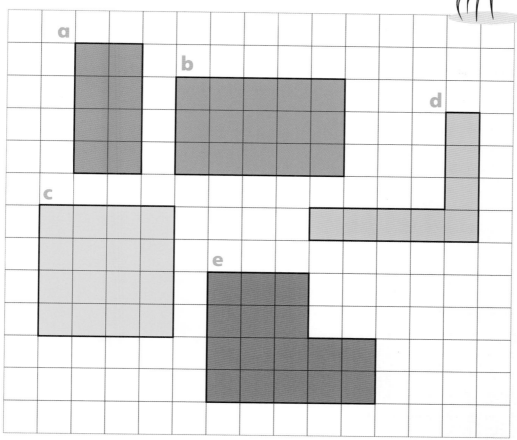

1. Shape a = ☐ squares
2. Shape b = ☐ squares
3. Shape c = ☐ squares
4. Shape d = ☐ squares
5. Shape e = ☐ squares

 **THINK** Draw a square with sides of 5 cm. What is its perimeter?

I am confident with measuring perimeters of squares and rectangles by counting centimetre squares.

Write the length of each side in squares.
Calculate the perimeter.

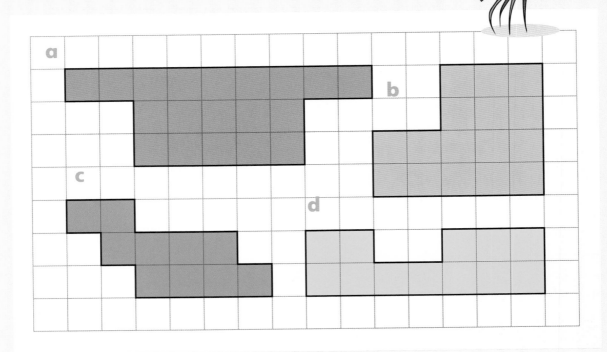

1. Shape a = ☐ squares

2. Shape b = ☐ squares

3. Shape c = ☐ squares

4. Shape d = ☐ squares

Measure each side of each shape.
Calculate the perimeter.

5.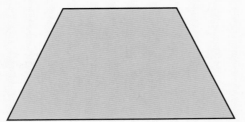

6.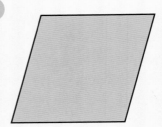

 Draw a square with sides of 7 cm.
What is its perimeter?

🔘 I am confident with measuring perimeters on
🔘 squared paper and using a ruler.

Work out the perimeter of each shape.

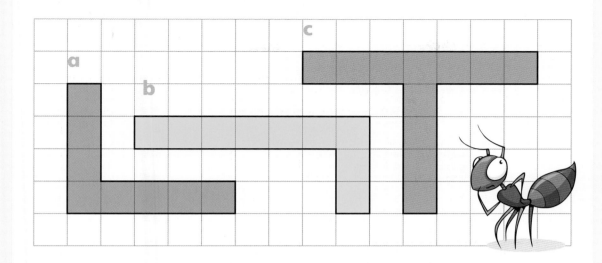

1   a = ☐ cm   2   b = ☐ cm   3   c = ☐ cm

Measure each side of each shape below. Calculate the perimeter.

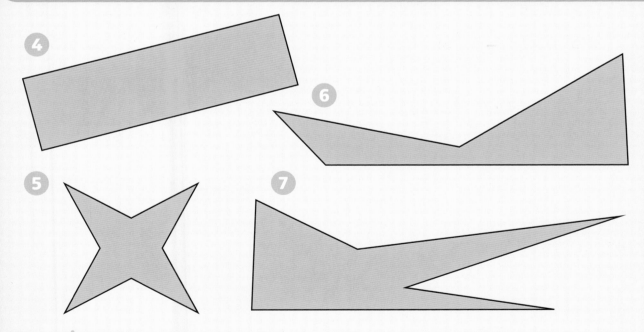

4

5

6

7

 **THINK**   Draw a shape with five sides. Measure the sides and find the perimeter to the nearest centimetre.

I am confident with measuring perimeters on squared paper and using a ruler.

Telling the time

Write each time as an analogue time in words.

1

4

7

2

5

8

3

6

9

Draw hands on clock faces to show these times.

10 Half past 6

11 Quarter to 8

12 Quarter past 9

13 Ten minutes past 2

14 Five minutes to 7

15 Twenty minutes to 4

THINK The minute hand of a clock is pointing to 3.
Write in words four different times it could be.

I am confident with telling the time to the nearest 5 minutes.

Write the matching digital time.

1   5   9

2   6   10

3   7   11

4   8   12

Write am or pm beside each time.

13   **I am walking to school.**   8:45

14   **I am going to bed.**   8:00

15   **I am having my lunch.**   12:30

THINK   Emily is doing an activity that you do every day. A time is showing on her watch. This time could be am or pm. Write what the time could be, and say what Emily could be doing. For example, she could be cleaning her teeth at 7:30.

I am confident with telling the time and using am and pm.

Write the matching digital time.

1.

5.

9.

2.

6.

10.

3.

7.

11.

4.

8.

12.

Draw the matching clock-face time and write am or pm beside each digital time.

13. I am walking to school.

8:30

14. I am eating my dinner.

7:00

15. I am playing football.

4:20

THINK It is 7:15. Write three things that you might be doing at 7:15 am or 7:15 pm.

I am confident with telling the time and using am and pm.

Draw an analogue clock to show the time 10 minutes later than the following times.

1. 11:20
2. 9:30
3. 12:10
4. 6:05
5. 2:35

6. 12:55
7. 4:40
8. 7:15
9. 1:50
10. 3:25

GRAB! Resource sheet of blank clock faces

Write the digital time when the activity ends.

It will take me 20 minutes to eat my dinner.

She will finish eating at 5:50.

5:30

11

I will play tennis for 40 minutes.

2:00

12

It will take 5 minutes to brush my teeth.

7:45

13

I am going to watch TV for 30 minutes.

4:15

THINK An activity takes 20 minutes and ends at half past 12. At what time did it start?

I am confident with working out the time a number of minutes later than a given time.

73

Draw an analogue clock to show the time 20 minutes later.

 GRAB! Resource sheet of blank clock faces

1. 4:15
2. 6:20
3. 7:40
4. 3:05

5. 12:30
6. 2:50
7. 8:10
8. 5:45

9. 11:55
10. 1:45
11. 9:55
12. 12:00

Write the time after each activity is finished. Write am or pm.

It will take me 15 minutes to walk to school.

8:30

He will get to school at 8:45 am.

13.

I will play this computer game for 20 minutes.

4:30

15.

I will play in the park for 30 minutes.

3:45

14.

It will take me 10 minutes to finish my breakfast.

7:30

16.

I am going to swim for 50 minutes.

11:30

THINK An activity takes 20 minutes and ends at quarter past 12. At what time did it start?

I am confident with working out the time a number of minutes later than a given time.

Multiplying 2-digit numbers by 1-digit numbers

Complete these multiplications.

1 5 × 32 = ☐

×	30	2
5	150	

= ☐

2 6 × 25 = ☐

×	20	5
6	120	

= ☐

3 9 × 23 = ☐

5 7 × 35 = ☐

4 8 × 34 = ☐

6 6 × 42 = ☐

 **THINK** How many answers did you get that were between 100 and 200? How many were between 200 and 300?

Write a multiplication ☐ × ☐☐ which gives an answer over 300.

○
○ **I am confident with multiplying 2-digit numbers**
○ **by 1-digit numbers using the grid method.**

Use Chunky Chimp to work out these divisions.

1 48 ÷ 4 = ☐

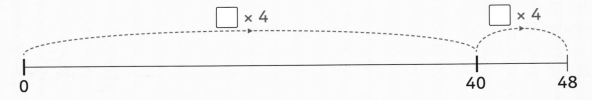

☐ × 4   ☐ × 4

0   40   48

2 44 ÷ 3 = ☐ r ☐

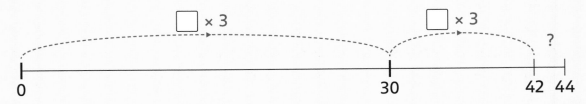

☐ × 3   ☐ × 3   ?

0   30   42 44

3 72 ÷ 5 = ☐ r ☐

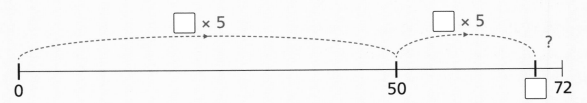

☐ × 5   ☐ × 5   ?

0   50   ☐ 72

4 54 ÷ 3 = ☐   **7** 74 ÷ 4 = ☐

5 64 ÷ 4 = ☐   **8** 95 ÷ 8 = ☐

6 94 ÷ 5 = ☐

THINK Choose three of these calculations and check the answers using multiplication.

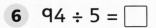
I am confident with dividing 2-digit numbers by 1-digit numbers using the chunking method.

Multiplication and division problems

Solve these word problems. Decide whether to use multiplication or division to find the answer.

1. There are 6 spiders in the bathroom. How many legs are there altogether?

2. Hannah counts 64 spider legs. How many spiders are there?

3. Jess reads 5 pages a day. How long will it take her to read a book that is 60 pages long?

4. Manjit reads 4 pages a day for 13 days and finishes his book. How long was the book?

5. Eleni pays £16 per month for broadband. How much does she pay for 3 months of broadband?

6. Sam pays £68 for 4 months of broadband. How much is this per month?

THINK Make up your own word problem for 14 × 5.

○
○   **I am confident with using multiplication and**
○   **division to solve word problems.**

Solve these word problems.

Remember to use RNCA!

1. 24 fish are caught in a net. The chef needs 8 fish to make a fish pie. How many pies can the chef make from today's catch? If a pie feeds 10 people, how many people can the chef cook for?

2. The next day, 56 fish are caught in the net. How many pies can the chef make from this catch? How many people can the chef cook for?

3. Chews cost 12p each. Mrs Jones buys one chew for each of her 8 children. How much change does she get from £1?

4. Mr Robson buys some 6p sweets. He has 85p. He wants to give 2 sweets each to his 7 children. Does he have enough money and if so, will he get change?

5. Each table in a classroom has 4 small chairs around it, apart from the teacher's table which has only one large chair. There are 17 tables in the classroom altogether. How many small chairs are there? If half of them are not empty, how many are empty?

6. In a different classroom there are 78 chairs. If 5 chairs are put round each table, leaving 3 chairs over, how many tables are there altogether?

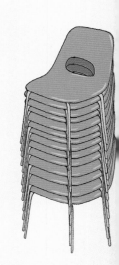

THINK Work with a partner to write two word problems like these.

I am confident with using multiplication and division to solve word problems.

Tenths and equivalent fractions

Write the fraction for each colour.

GRAB! Sticks of 10 in red and blue

1 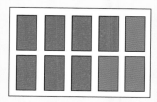 red = $\frac{\square}{10}$

blue = $\frac{\square}{10}$

4 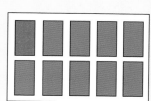 red = $\frac{\square}{10}$

blue = $\frac{\square}{10}$

2 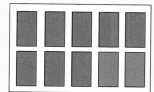 red = $\frac{\square}{10}$

blue = $\frac{\square}{10}$

5 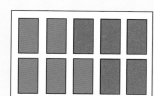 red = $\frac{\square}{10}$

blue = $\frac{\square}{10}$

3 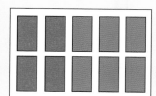 red = $\frac{\square}{10}$

blue = $\frac{\square}{10}$

6 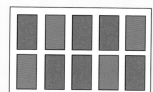 red = $\frac{\square}{10}$

blue = $\frac{\square}{10}$

7 Which sheet of stickers has one-half in red?

8 Which sheet of stickers has one-fifth in blue?

THINK Write an addition of three fractions which gives the answer 1.

I am confident with tenths.

Write the number of red tiles as a fraction.
If you can, write the fraction in another way.

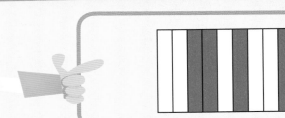 $= \dfrac{4}{10} = \dfrac{2}{5}$

①

④

②

⑤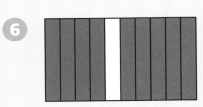

③

⑥

Write < or > between each pair of fractions.

⑦ $\dfrac{1}{10}$ $\dfrac{3}{10}$

⑨ $\dfrac{3}{10}$ $\dfrac{6}{10}$

⑪ $\dfrac{7}{10}$ $\dfrac{1}{2}$

⑧ $\dfrac{1}{2}$ $\dfrac{6}{10}$

⑩ $\dfrac{1}{5}$ $\dfrac{3}{10}$

 **THINK** Write an addition of two fractions which equal I, where the denominator in each fraction is different.

I am confident with tenths and equivalent fractions.

1. $\frac{1}{10}$ of 50p = ☐ p

2. $\frac{3}{10}$ of 50p = ☐ p

3. $\frac{2}{10}$ of 50p = ☐ p

4. $\frac{9}{10}$ of 50p = ☐ p

5. $\frac{1}{10}$ of 40 = ☐

   $\frac{3}{10}$ of 40 = ☐

6. $\frac{1}{10}$ of 70 = ☐

   $\frac{2}{10}$ of 70 = ☐

7. $\frac{1}{10}$ of 80 = ☐

   $\frac{3}{10}$ of 80 = ☐

8. $\frac{1}{10}$ of 120 = ☐

   $\frac{4}{10}$ of 120 = ☐

9. $\frac{1}{10}$ of 250 = ☐

   $\frac{6}{10}$ of 250 = ☐

10. $\frac{1}{10}$ of 100 = ☐

    $\frac{5}{10}$ of 100 = ☐

11. $\frac{1}{10}$ of 1000 = ☐

    $\frac{7}{10}$ of 1000 = ☐

12. $\frac{1}{10}$ of 130 = ☐

    $\frac{8}{10}$ of 130 = ☐

 **THINK** Which is bigger: $\frac{1}{10}$ of 450 or $\frac{1}{2}$ of 100?

1 $\frac{1}{10}$ of 70 = ☐

$\frac{3}{10}$ of 70 = ☐

2 $\frac{1}{10}$ of 50 = ☐

$\frac{5}{10}$ of 50 = ☐

3 $\frac{1}{10}$ of 30 = ☐

$\frac{8}{10}$ of 30 = ☐

4 $\frac{1}{10}$ of 150 = ☐

$\frac{3}{10}$ of 150 = ☐

5 $\frac{1}{10}$ of 120 = ☐

$\frac{4}{10}$ of 120 = ☐

6 $\frac{1}{10}$ of 320 = ☐

$\frac{2}{10}$ of 320 = ☐

7 $\frac{1}{10}$ of 200 = ☐

$\frac{9}{10}$ of 200 = ☐

8 $\frac{1}{10}$ of 440 = ☐

$\frac{2}{10}$ of 440 = ☐

9 $\frac{1}{10}$ of 500 = ☐

$\frac{3}{10}$ of 500 = ☐

10 $\frac{1}{10}$ of 360 = ☐

$\frac{8}{10}$ of 360 = ☐

11 In one of these questions you found $\frac{1}{2}$ of a number. How do you write $\frac{1}{2}$ in tenths?

THINK If $\frac{6}{10}$ = 60, what is $\frac{1}{10}$? What number are we finding tenths of?

I am confident with finding tenths of 2- and 3-digit numbers.

Find one-tenth of each number.

1 50

2 60

3 240

4 120

5 80

6 320

7 110

8 900

Find three-tenths of each number.

9 90

10 120

11 140

12 200

Find the following fractions.

13 $\frac{4}{10}$ of 60

14 $\frac{9}{10}$ of 50

15 $\frac{7}{10}$ of 110

16 $\frac{3}{10}$ of 70

THINK Write $\frac{1}{10}$ of 20, $\frac{2}{10}$ of 30, $\frac{3}{10}$ of 40, $\frac{4}{10}$ of 50. Keep going to $\frac{9}{10}$ of 100. What pattern do you notice in the answers? Can you describe this pattern?

I am confident with finding tenths of 2- and 3-digit numbers.

Add the multiples of 10 mentally. Complete the second addition using column addition.

1. 240 + 150 + 300 = ☐

   248 + 157 + 302 = ☐

2. 330 + 150 + 400 = ☐

   338 + 159 + 407 = ☐

3. 140 + 160 + 200 = ☐

   147 + 166 + 208 = ☐

4. 380 + 210 + 400 = ☐

   388 + 216 + 404 = ☐

5. 240 + 140 + 300 = ☐

   247 + 148 + 309 = ☐

What is the difference between the answers?

Is there a quick way to work out the second addition?

 **THINK** Write three more pairs of additions like these, with 3-digit multiples of 10 in the first addition. In the second addition, the same 100s and 10s digits as the first addition, but with 1s digits that will add up to more than 10. Swap additions with a partner and solve them.

 I am confident with adding 3-digit numbers using mental and written methods.

Use Frog to work out these subtractions.

1. $200 - 121 = \square$

2. $300 - 232 = \square$

3. $400 - 343 = \square$

4. $500 - 454 = \square$

5. $600 - 565 = \square$

6. $700 - 676 = \square$

7. $800 - 787 = \square$

8. What might the next question be?
   What will the answer be?

Use Frog to work out these subtractions.

9. $900 - 876 = \square$

10. $800 - 765 = \square$

11. $700 - 654 = \square$

12. $600 - 543 = \square$

 **THINK** Continue the pattern with three more questions and answers.

I am confident with subtracting 3-digit numbers by counting up.

1   212 – 121 = ☐

2   323 – 232 = ☐

3   434 – 343 = ☐

4   545 – 454 = ☐

5   Write four more subtractions that follow the pattern and answer them.

6   What do you notice about the answers?

Use Frog to work out these subtractions. The digits next to each other in each number have a difference of 2.

7   313 – 131 = ☐

8   424 – 242 = ☐

9   535 – 353 = ☐

10   Write down and work out the next two subtractions in this pattern. What do you notice about the answers?

 Write some subtractions like these but where the digits in each number have a difference of 3, such as 414 – 141. What do you notice about the answers?

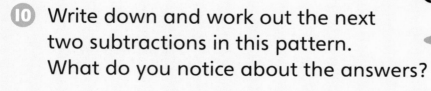 **I am confident with subtracting 3-digit numbers.**

Work out how much change you would get from £10 for each of these meals.

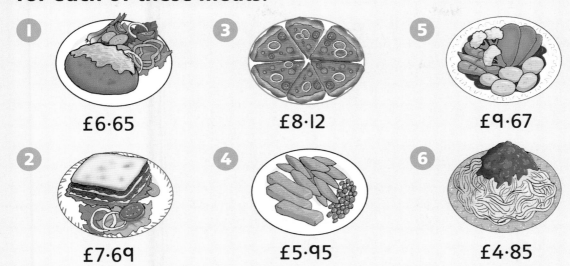

1 £6·65	**3** £8·12	**5** £9·67
2 £7·69	**4** £5·95	**6** £4·85

Work out how much change you would get from £20 for each of these meal deals.

7 Menu
Meal Deal
Any starter and Main for just
£12·55

9 COME TO
GOOD GRUB
ONLY
ONLY £14·65
£14·65
for a main course and dessert
SPECIAL

11 MENU
Posh Nosh Deal
£17·89
for two courses

8 Menu
CHOOSE A MAIN AND A DESSERT FOR
£13·78

10
Meal Deal!
£11·97

12 Menu
Enjoy TWO courses for
£15·42

THINK Choose three of these subtractions.
Check the answers by using addition.

○
○
○ **I am confident with working out change from £10 and £20 by counting up.**

Use the grid method for each multiplication.

$4 \times 24p = \square$

× 4

×	20	4	
4	80	16	96

= 96p

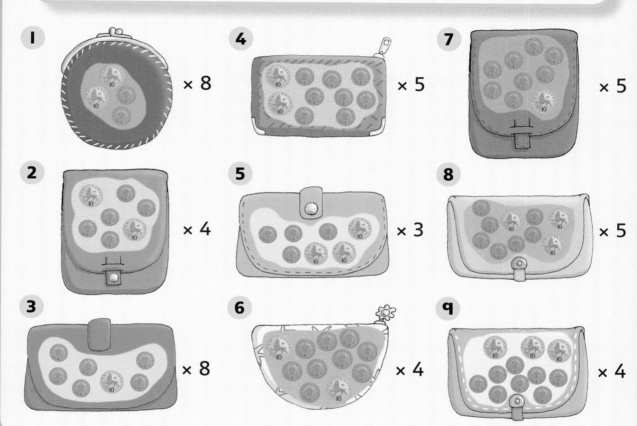

1. × 8

2. × 4

3. × 8

4. × 5

5. × 3

6. × 4

7. × 5

8. × 5

9. × 4

3	4	2

THINK How many $\square\square \times \square$ calculations can you write using only these digit cards? Try to find them all. Which has the largest answer? Which has the smallest answer?

I am confident with multiplying 2-digit numbers by 1-digit numbers using the grid method.

Complete these multiplications using the 24 times-table.

1   1 × 24 = 24

2   2 × 24 = ☐

3   3 × 24 = ☐

4   4 × 24 = ☐

5   5 × 24 = ☐

6   8 × 24 = ☐

7   Add the answers to questions 1 and 2 to check your answer to question 3.

8   Add the answers to questions 2 and 3 to check your answer to question 5.

9   Double your answer to question 4 to check your answer to question 8.

Use your answers to questions 1 to 6 to complete these facts from the 24 times-table.

10   6 × 24 = ☐

11   7 × 24 = ☐

12   9 × 24 = ☐

13   10 × 24 = ☐

You can double the answer to Question 3 to find one of these facts.

What fact would you find if you add the answers to Question 3 and Question 4?

THINK   Is 3 × 42 the same answer as 4 × 32? Is 5 × 34 the same as 3 × 54? What about 4 × 38 and 3 × 48?

I am confident with working out the 24 times-table.

Dividing using a number line

Complete these divisions using number lines.

1 85 ÷ 5 = ☐

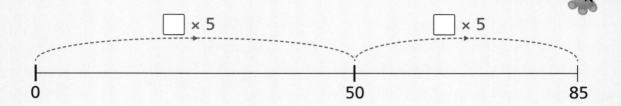

☐ × 5   ☐ × 5

0   50   85

2 48 ÷ 3 = ☐

5 54 ÷ 3 = ☐

3 64 ÷ 4 = ☐

6 88 ÷ 4 = ☐

4 90 ÷ 5 = ☐

7 104 ÷ 8 = ☐

Complete these divisions and find the remainder in each case.

8 54 ÷ 4 = ☐ r ☐

10 63 ÷ 4 = ☐ r ☐

9 73 ÷ 3 = ☐ r ☐

11 89 ÷ 3 = ☐ r ☐

THINK Work out 45 ÷ 3. Then write the answers to 46 ÷ 3 and 47 ÷ 3 without doing any more work!

I am confident with dividing 2-digit numbers by 1-digit numbers using a number line.

Complete these divisions.

1 85 ÷ 5 = ☐

2 51 ÷ 3 = ☐

3 66 ÷ 4 = ☐

4 92 ÷ 5 = ☐

5 57 ÷ 3 = ☐

6 104 ÷ 8 = ☐

7 54 ÷ 4 = ☐

8 53 ÷ 3 = ☐

9 63 ÷ 4 = ☐

10 108 ÷ 8 = ☐

Solve these word problems.

11 Molly has a collection of 55 small china ornaments. She wants to tidy them into boxes. 4 ornaments fit in each box. How many boxes will she need?

12 Jamil has a party for his birthday. He wants to make a toy tricycle for each friend coming. He has 58 wheels. How many toy tricycles can he make?

 **THINK** Work out 112 ÷ 8. Say the answers to 115 ÷ 8 and 120 ÷ 8 without doing any more work!

I am confident with dividing 2-digit numbers by 1-digit numbers using a number line.

Practising calculations

Use mental methods.

1 863 – 40 = ☐

2 747 + 80 = ☐

3 708 + 84 = ☐

4 624 + 239 = ☐

5 543 + 60 = ☐

6 361 – 80 = ☐

7 444 + 38 = ☐

8 354 + 171 = ☐

Use the grid method for these.

9 3 × 24 = ☐

10 5 × 33 = ☐

11 8 × 26 = ☐

12 4 × 19 = ☐

13 3 × 42 = ☐

14 7 × 43 = ☐

Use written methods for these.

15
```
   529
+  347
─────
```

16
```
   281
   163
+  392
─────
```

17
```
    42
    76
    58
+   26
─────
```

18
```
   324
+  288
─────
```

19
```
   392
   354
+  216
─────
```

20
```
    74
    83
    48
+  126
─────
```

Use a number line or Frog for these.

21 $763 - 717 = \square$

22 $68 \div 4 = \square$

23 $90 \div 5 = \square$

24 $54 \div 4 = \square$

25 $727 - 681 = \square$

26 $128 \div 8 = \square$

27 $76 \div 4 = \square$

28 $58 \div 3 = \square$

Choose any suitable method for each of these.

29 $434 + 247 = \square$

30 $642 + 128 = \square$

31 $48 + 37 = \square$

32 $483 + 111 = \square$

33 $140 + 160 + 200 = \square$

34 $535 - 353 = \square$

35 $52 \div 3 = \square$ r $\square$

36 $17 \times 5 = \square$

37 $674 + 288 = \square$

38 $467 + 217 = \square$

39 $736 + 150 = \square$

40 $385 + 261 = \square$

41 $424 - 242 = \square$

42 $247 + 148 + 309 = \square$

43 $95 \div 5 = \square$

44 $16 \times 6 = \square$

Solve these problems.

45 Chews cost 12p each. Mrs Lee buys one chew for each of her 8 children. How much change from £1 does she get?

46 Ron has 62 gold coins, Ben has 82 and Jo has 74. If they find 89 more, how many coins do they have in total?

Fraction puzzles

There are 12 children in a photo. Read clues about them.

$\frac{1}{2}$ of the children are girls and $\frac{2}{4}$ are boys

$\frac{1}{4}$ of the children are waving

$\frac{4}{4}$ of the children are smiling

$\frac{1}{3}$ of them are wearing scarves

$\frac{3}{4}$ of them are wearing hats

$\frac{5}{6}$ of the girls are wearing skirts

$\frac{2}{3}$ of the boys are holding footballs

1 Draw a picture of the 12 children so that each clue is true.

2 You could write fraction clues of your own.

3

Use the digits 2, 4, 1 and 8.
Make as many different fraction questions
and answers as you can using them all.

How many true statements
can you find?

$\frac{1}{4}$ of 8 = 2

4 What fraction of the group are wearing hats?

5 What fraction are wearing glasses?

6 What fraction are smiling?

7 Write two equivalent fractions to show what fraction are not smiling.

8 What fraction of the group has glasses but no hat?

9 Write two equivalent fractions to show what fraction are wearing hats and smiling.

The hour hand is missing from this clock-face.

- At 1 o'clock the hour hand would be $\frac{1}{12}$ of the way around the clock face.

- At 2 o'clock the hour hand would be $\frac{2}{12}$ or $\frac{1}{6}$ the way around the clock face.

10 For each of the other o'clock times, write what fraction of the circle the hour hand would be around the circle. Write equivalent fractions, where possible.

Series Editor
Ruth Merttens

Author Team
Jennie Kerwin and Hilda Merttens

Published by Pearson Education Limited, Edinburgh Gate, Harlow, Essex, CM20 2JE.

www.pearsonschools.co.uk

Text © Pearson Education Limited 2014
Page design and layout by room9design
Original illustrations © Pearson Education Limited 2014
Illustrated by Andrew Roland pp10–11, 16–18, 24–26, 30, 32–35, 50–53, 56–60, 71–74, 77–79, 87–88, 91; Matt Buckley
pp 9, 21–26, 31–32, 35, 49, 55–57, 64–72, 76, 90, 95; Andrew Painter pp13–15, 33; Marek Jagucki pp21, 24, 67–69, 76, 90
Cover design by Pearson Education Limited
Cover illustration and Abacus character artwork by Volker Beisler © Pearson Education Limited
Additional contributions by Hilary Koll and Steve Mills, CME Projects Ltd.

First published 2014

2019
10

British Library Cataloguing in Publication Data
A catalogue record for this book is available from the British Library

ISBN 978 1 408 27849 9

Printed in Great Britain by Bell and Bain Ltd, Glasgow

Acknowledgements
We would like to thank the staff and pupils at North Kidlington Primary School, Haydon Wick Primary School, Swindon, St Mary's Catholic Primary School, Bodmin, St Andrew's C of E Primary & Nursery School, Sutton-in-Ashfield, Saint James' C of E Primary School, Southampton and Harborne Primary School, Birmingham, for their invaluable help in the development and trialling of this book.

Every effort has been made to contact copyright holders of material reproduced in this book. Any omissions will be rectified in subsequent printings if notice is given to the publishers.